Clever
Kids

Science
Ages 5-7

World Book, Inc.
Chicago London Sydney Toronto

World Book, Inc.
525 W. Monroe
Chicago, IL 60661

For information on other World Book products, call 1-800-255-1750.

ISBN: 0-7166-9204-X
LC: 95-61314

Printed in Mexico

2 3 4 5 6 7 8 9 10 99 98 97 96 95

Contents

That's Life

YOU NEED:

* ★ Sand or soil
* ★ A baking pan
* ★ Sticks, dried leaves, and stones
* ★ Construction paper
* ★ Seeds

You're alive! How do you know? You grow. You need food, water, and air.

You are a person, like other people in your family. Your children will be people, like you.

Which of these things are also alive?

Living things grow. They can make other living things that look and behave like themselves. And they need food, air, and water to do these things.

Can you name some other living things? Can you name some things that are not living?

4

SCIENCE NOTE
You can use grass seed, flower seeds (for small plants), and even birdseed to make a baking-pan garden with living plants. A layer of gravel or charcoal in the bottom of the pan will improve drainage. Don't overwater.

You can make a baking-pan garden. It can look like a garden with living things, or it can have real living things in it.

1. Put a layer of sand or soil about 1 inch (2.5 centimeters) deep in the bottom of the baking pan. If you have some pretty stones, put them in, too.

2. Make some plants for your garden. Use sticks, dried weeds, and other things you find that remind you of plants. You can also make plants from construction paper.

3. Make some other things to put in your garden. For example, make a path with stones or sand. Use a small mirror for a pond.

4. Look at your garden. How is it like a real garden? How is it different? Are there any living things in it?

5. Make another baking-pan garden with living things or change the one you've made. Try planting grass seeds, flower seeds, or birdseed. Don't forget that your plants will need air, water, and sunlight to grow.

Plant Parts

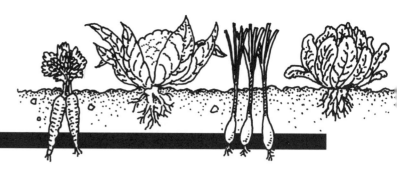

A plant can't jump rope, roller-skate, read, or eat a hot dog. But it can do some things that you and all other living things do. You use different parts of your body to do the things you can do. A plant uses its parts to do things, too.

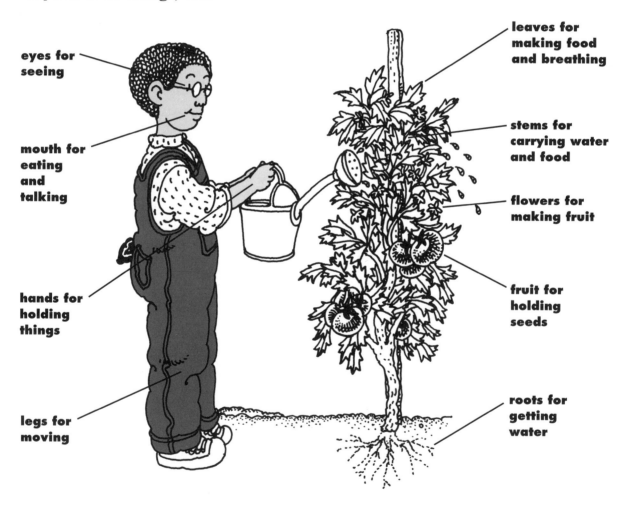

eyes for seeing

mouth for eating and talking

hands for holding things

legs for moving

leaves for making food and breathing

stems for carrying water and food

flowers for making fruit

fruit for holding seeds

roots for getting water

Plants are also food for people. Do you know how many kinds of plant parts you can eat? Every kind there is!

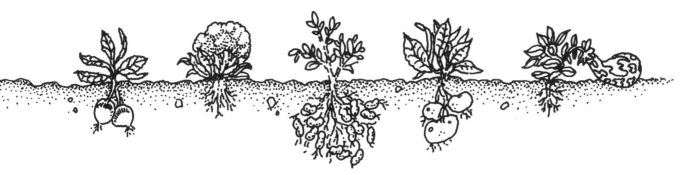

Activity 1: Figure It Out

★ Pictured above are some plants you can eat. Do you know what they are? See below for answers.

★ On your next trip to the grocery store, look at the fruits and vegetables. Try to find plants with different parts you can eat—for example, roots, stems, flowers, and seeds. Are there any plants you eat more than one part of?

Activity 2: These Veggies Were Made for Snackin'

★ Raw vegetables make good snacks. You can break up broccoli, cut up carrots and celery, and slice cucumbers. Ask a grown-up to help you do these things. What other vegetables can you snack on?

★ Eat your veggie snack plain, or make a dip. Stir a teaspoon of honey or salad dressing into a cup of plain yogurt. Dip the vegetable before you take a bite. Yum!

Plants, from left to right: carrots, cauliflower, onions, lettuce, beets, broccoli, peanuts, potatoes, squash.

A Green Thumb, and Fingers

YOU NEED:

★ Several kinds of seeds
★ Water
★ A knife
★ Potting soil
★ 3 clear plastic cups
★ Scissors
★ Black construction paper
★ Tape

How does a seed grow into a plant? Here is what happens to one kind of seed. What part grows first? Next? After that?

Think about what the plant will look like when it grows bigger than the last picture shown. How will it change?

Get to the root of seeds and how they grow into plants by doing these two activities.

Activity 1: Look at Seeds

1. Save some seeds from uncooked fruits and vegetables. Or, buy packages of garden seeds.

2. Pick out one of each kind of seed. How are they alike? How are they different? Do you think they will be the same or different inside?

3. Soak the seeds in water for a few minutes. Then have a grown-up help you cut or break them open. Are they alike or different inside?

Activity 2: Watch Seeds Grow

1. Put some potting soil in the plastic cups. Fill them almost full.

2. Pick three kinds of seeds. (Big seeds are the easiest to watch.) Plant each kind in a plastic cup. Put two seeds in each cup, next to the outside, so you can see them through the cup.

3. Cut a piece of the black construction paper as wide as the cup is high. Wrap it around the cup and tape it. Then water your seeds. What do you think you will see when the seeds begin to grow? Do you think the same things will happen to each kind of seed?

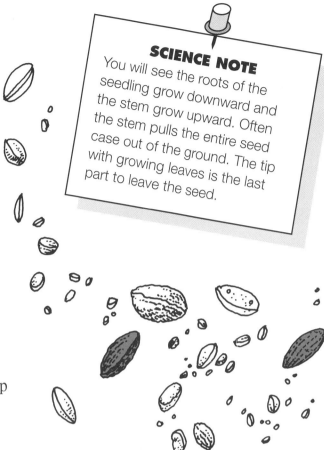

SCIENCE NOTE
You will see the roots of the seedling grow downward and the stem grow upward. Often the stem pulls the entire seed case out of the ground. The tip with growing leaves is the last part to leave the seed.

4. Every day, take the paper off and look at the seeds. Are the seeds growing the way you thought they would?

9

Animals Alive!

Take a look at the animals in this picture. You'll find many different ones. But look closely and you'll find that they are alike in some ways.

SCIENCE NOTE

Insects, as well as spiders, centipedes, crabs, and other creatures with many legs, belong to a group of animals called arthropods. Snails, like clams, oysters, and many other animals with shells, are mollusks.

Most mammals have hair or fur, and all mammals feed their babies milk. Which animals in this picture are mammals?

Birds have feathers and lay eggs. How many birds do you see?

Reptiles have scaly skin and lay eggs. How many reptiles can you find?

Now find some other animals in this picture. How are they different from mammals, birds, or reptiles?

Fish have *gills*—curved, thin openings on their sides, just behind their heads. They breathe underwater through their gills. How many fish do you see?

Amphibians live in two places. When they are small, they have gills and live in the water. When they grow up, they have lungs and live on land. Do you see any amphibians in this picture?

What a **T**reat!

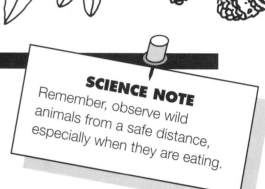

YOU NEED:
* ★ Peanut butter
* ★ A pine cone or corncob
* ★ Birdseed
* ★ String
* ★ A knife
* ★ A bagel or hard roll

SCIENCE NOTE
Remember, observe wild animals from a safe distance, especially when they are eating.

Think about all the different kinds of food you eat.

Which ones are your favorites? What do you enjoy

eating as an extra-special treat?

Believe it or not, animals like special treats, too. Here are some

treats you can make for the animals in your neighborhood.

Activity 1: Animal Lollipop

1. Make sure your peanut butter is room temperature. Spread some around the middle of the pine cone or corncob. Leave the ends bare so you can pick it up.

2. Roll the pine cone or corncob in seed until the peanut butter is covered.

3. Tie a short length of string to one end of the pine cone or corncob and hang your treat in a bush or tree.

4. What kind of animal do you think will enjoy your treat? How do you think the animal will eat it? Make a chart of your predictions. Then watch what happens. Place a treat on the ground to see if it attracts different animals.

Activity 2: Who's Having Lunch?

1. Have a grown-up help you slice a bagel or hard roll in half lengthwise. Spread both sides with peanut butter and cover them with birdseed.

2. Tie some string through the hole in the bagel or around the middle of the hard roll. Hang the treat in a bush or tree.

3. Do you think the same kinds of animals will like this treat? Do you think they will eat it in the same way? Watch what happens and see.

There's No Place Like Home

YOU NEED:

★ A large sheet of paper
★ A paper plate
★ Crayons
★ Scissors
★ Old magazines

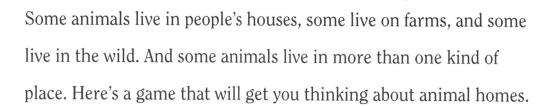

Some animals live in people's houses, some live on farms, and some

live in the wild. And some animals live in more than one kind of

place. Here's a game that will get you thinking about animal homes.

1. On the large sheet of paper, trace
around the plate with a crayon three
times to make a design like the one
shown here. Use a different color for
each circle. Make sure the circles
overlap.

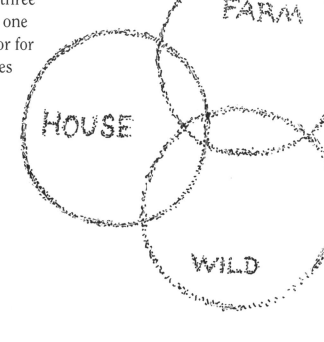

2. Print *farm* in one circle, *house* in another, and *wild* in the third. Or, draw a picture of each place. Be careful not to draw where the circles overlap. This kind of drawing is called a Venn diagram.

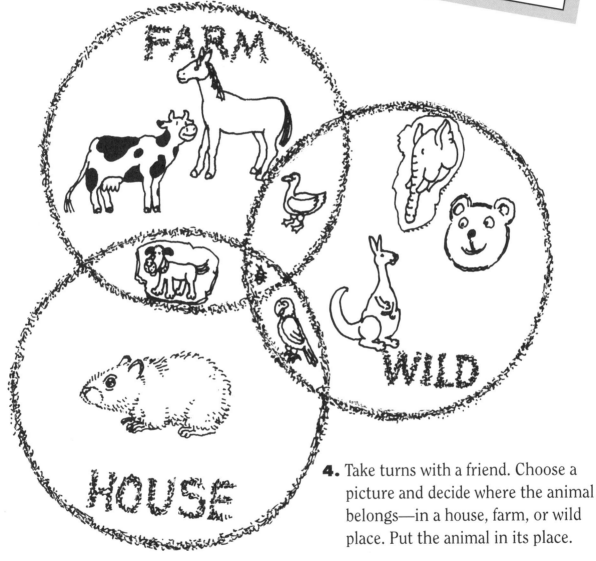

3. Cut pictures of different kinds of animals from old magazines. (Make sure you get permission first from whoever owns the magazines.) Now you are ready to play.

4. Take turns with a friend. Choose a picture and decide where the animal belongs—in a house, farm, or wild place. Put the animal in its place.

5. If an animal could live in two places, put it where the two circles overlap. If it could live in all three places, put it in the middle. Explain why you put it in one of those places.

Rock'n **D**iscoveries

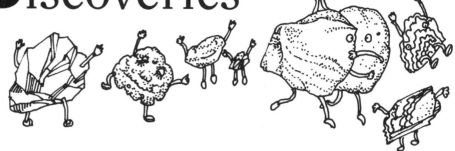

YOU NEED:
- ★ A variety of rocks
- ★ An egg carton
- ★ A butter knife

What makes a rock so rocky? How did it get to be hard? Rocks can be made in different ways, and they can be made of many different materials.

Sandstone is grains of sand that have stuck together to make rock.

Marble is rock that was formed from another kind of rock. Heating and squeezing caused it to change.

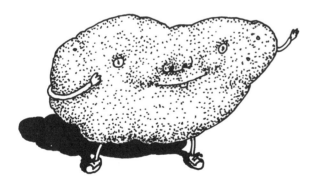

Granite is rock that got heated deep in the earth. It's very hard.

SCIENCE NOTE
Good places to look for rocks include beaches, gravel roads, and garden soil as well as rocky ground. Museum shops often sell rocks.

Here are some things you can do with rocks:

Activity 1: Be a Rock Hound

1. Look in places near your home for different kinds of rocks. See how many you can find.

2. Wash each rock. See how it looks when it's wet and when it's dry.

3. Study each rock. Does it have layers? Does it have shiny crystals? Is it rough or smooth?

4. Store your rocks in the egg carton and show them to your friends.

Activity 2: Give the Rocks a Test

1. Feel each rock that you found in Activity 1 with your fingernail. Do you think each would scratch a sidewalk? Try it and see whether they do or not.

2. Get permission from a grown-up to use an old butter knife. Which rocks do you think the knife will scratch? Try it.

3. Which rocks are smoothest? Which are roughest? Arrange the rocks in the egg carton so all the smooth ones are in one row and all the rough ones are in the other row.

17

It's in the Dirt!

YOU NEED:

★ A digging tool
★ A few spoonfuls of soil
★ A paper towel
★ A magnifying glass
★ A spoon
★ A jar with a lid
★ Water

That's not just dirt under your feet—it's the soil that plants need to grow. What do you think it's made of? How many things do you see in the picture above that go into soil?

Dig in your heels and get the dirt on dirt.

Activity 1: Dig In!

1. Dig up a bit of soil from the ground around your home. Or, use a little potting soil that's used for house plants. (Make sure you get permission first.)

2. Spread a spoonful of the soil on a paper towel. Look at the soil through the magnifying glass. Do all the bits of soil look the same, or are some of them different? What do they look like?

18

Activity 2: Test Your Soil

1. Put two spoonfuls of soil in a jar. Fill the jar with water and screw the lid on tight.

2. Shake the jar over a sink for 30 seconds to mix the soil and water. Then set the jar down. How much soil is in the bottom? Is any of it floating?

3. Wait 15 minutes. Then look at your soil again. How much is on the bottom of the jar now? Does all of it look alike, or are the layers different? What do they look like?

4. Test samples of soil from different places, such as your yard, the schoolyard, and the playground. Do you think all the samples will look the same or different? Try to guess what each sample will look like. Then test your samples in the jar to see what happens.

'Tis the Season

YOU NEED:

- ★ Paper
- ★ Crayons
- ★ A pencil
- ★ A shoebox
- ★ A sheet of construction paper
- ★ Glue or tape
- ★ Scissors

The four seasons are times of year that have a certain kind of weather—rainy or dry, cold or hot. Did you know that seasons can be different in different places? If you watch the weather, you can learn a lot about seasons where you live.

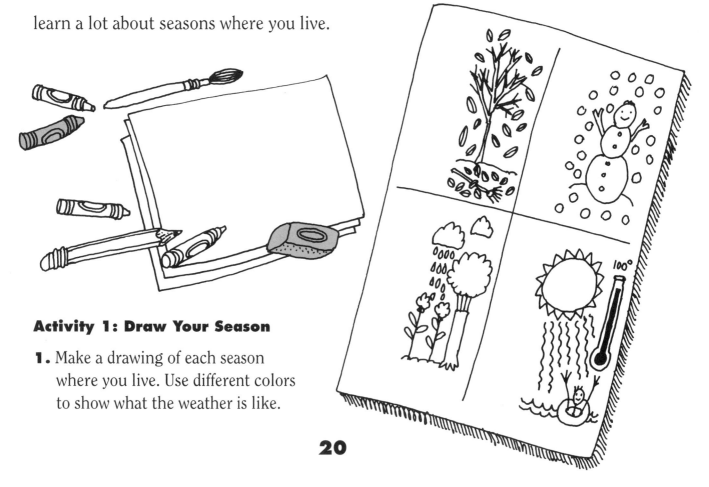

Activity 1: Draw Your Season

1. Make a drawing of each season where you live. Use different colors to show what the weather is like.

2. Below or beside each picture, make a list of the clothes you wear and the things you do in that season. Or, draw pictures to show what you wear and do.

3. Have you ever lived in a place, visited a place, or known someone who lives in a place where the weather during each season is different than where you live? Draw pictures to show the seasons in that place.

Activity 2: Collect a Season

1. What's your favorite season? Collect a box full of things that show what you like about it. Find real things, such as plants, bird feathers, or sea shells. Also, cut pictures from old magazines (ask permission first), or use pictures you draw.

2. Make a collage of your favorite season. Arrange some of the things you collected on the construction paper. When they are the way you like, glue them or tape them in place.

SCIENCE NOTE
Spring, summer, autumn, and winter are names we give to the four seasons. But many areas don't have four seasons, or don't have the kind of weather people think those seasons should have. Your project should be about seasons where you live.

Weather **M**ini-**F**orecast

YOU NEED:

★ A calendar (one that has squares for the days)
★ Crayons or colored pencils
★ A sheet of tracing paper

Take a look out a window. What is the weather today where you live? Is it snowing and blowing? Is the sun shining? Is it raining?

You can try your hand at forecasting, or predicting, the weather. Everything you need is right outside your window!

1. Watch the weather for a week. Draw a picture of it in the calendar square for each day. You might draw a sun, clouds, a raindrop, a snowflake, or a tree blowing in the wind. On some days, you may need to draw two or more things.

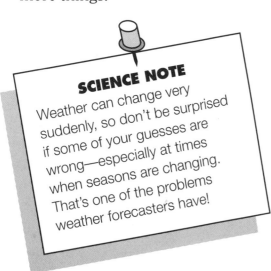

SCIENCE NOTE

Weather can change very suddenly, so don't be surprised if some of your guesses are wrong—especially at times when seasons are changing. That's one of the problems weather forecasters have!

2. After a week, look at the pictures you drew. Did the weather stay the same or did it change? If it changed, how did it change? Did it get warmer or colder? Did it get wetter or drier?

3. Now try to forecast what next week's weather will be. Tape the tracing paper over the next week on the calendar. Draw pictures to show your weather forecast for each day. Take the paper off and save it.

4. Watch the weather for the next week. Draw pictures on the calendar to show what the weather really is.

5. At the end of the week, compare your weather forecast with the real weather. Do you think you're ready to take over as the TV news weather forecaster?

Make Dew!

YOU NEED:

★ A wide-mouthed jar with a lid
★ Hot water
★ A paper towel
★ A dishtowel
★ A measuring spoon

On a cool morning, have you ever seen dew, which looks like tiny drops of water, on the grass and flowers? Dew forms when warm, damp air gets cool. You can make dew in your kitchen.

⚠ **Have a grown-up help with the hot water.**

1. Fill the jar with hot water. Screw on the lid. Let the jar sit until it feels warm to the touch on the outside.

2. Fold the paper towel until it is small enough to fit inside the jar.

3. When the jar is warm, pour out the water and dry it with the dishtowel. Make sure the sides are dry.

4. Now you need to work quickly. Wet the folded paper towel with warm water from the faucet and put it in the bottom of the jar. Place the spoon in the jar so it leans against the side. Screw the lid on tightly.

5. Put the jar in the refrigerator. Leave it for a half-hour. Then take it out. What does it look like? Open the jar and feel the inside. Is it damp or dry? Is the spoon dry?

SCIENCE NOTE

Warm air holds more water vapor than cold air. When warm air cools, some of the water vapor condenses—it comes out of the air and collects on things as dew.

Water-Go-Round

When you drink a glass of water, you know where the water came from—a faucet or a bottle. But how did it get to the faucet or bottle? And when you empty your water glass into the sink, you know where the water goes—down the drain. But then where does it go?

The water from your faucet isn't used just once. It travels from place to place and gets used again and again.

Look at this picture that shows how water can travel.

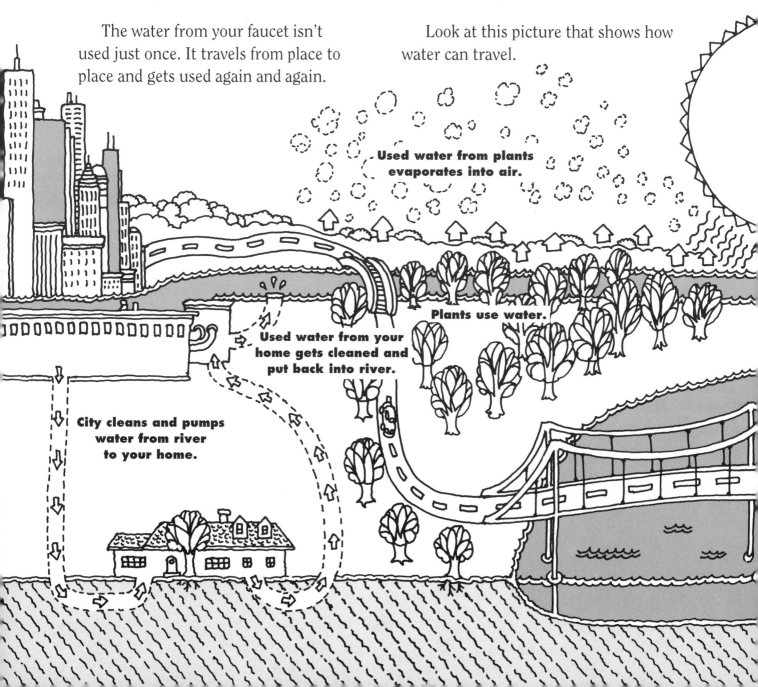

Used water from plants evaporates into air.

Plants use water.

Used water from your home gets cleaned and put back into river.

City cleans and pumps water from river to your home.

1. Find a way that water can get from the air to the ground.

2. Find two places water can go when it gets to the ground.

3. Find as many places as you can that the water in your home can come from.

4. Find two ways that water can get back into the air.

5. Find the way that the sun helps move water around.

SCIENCE NOTE
Try to find out where water in your area comes from. Are there rules about using water where you live? Try to find out why.

Imagine you are a drop of water. Tell or write a story about where you come from, how you are used, and how you get back to where you came from. You can make your water-drop trip as long or short as you like. You may want to draw pictures to go with your story.

Water vapor forms clouds.

Sun makes water evaporate from land.

Clouds rain on earth.

Sun makes water evaporate from river.

Rain soaks into earth.

Water sinks into ground.

Underground water flows into river.

It's in the **A**ir and **W**ater

YOU NEED:

* ★ Small, light objects
* ★ A paper fan, a straw, or other things you can use to move air
* ★ A smooth tabletop
* ★ One or two baking pans filled with water

You know what wind is. You can't see it, but you can feel it—it's moving air. And even though you can't see it, you can see what it does. What things in this picture let you know the wind is blowing?

Just like the wind, you can make things happen with moving air.

1. Find a small, light object, such as a cork, a feather, a piece of paper, or a small ball. Put it on the tabletop.

2. Now think of some ways to move it with air. Of course, you can use your breath. What other ways can you think of? Which do you think will work best?

3. Try all the ways you thought of. Decide which one works best.

4. Do this activity two or three times with different objects.

5. Now try this with a friend. Pick two objects that are exactly the same. Pick different ways to make it move. Have a race to see who can make it move across the table faster.

6. Next, get a baking pan full of water, two pans if you're doing this with a friend. Predict which ways you can best use air to move items across the water. Do you think the best way will be the same as for the tabletop? Try different ways and see. Then have you and your friend race to see who can move an item across the water faster.

SCIENCE NOTE
Use a smooth tabletop or counter or a long baking pan full of water for best results.

Where's the **W**ind?

YOU NEED:

- ★ A small plastic lid from a margarine tub or similar container
- ★ Scissors
- ★ A plastic bag just big enough to fit around the lid (a bread bag or newspaper bag)
- ★ Transparent tape

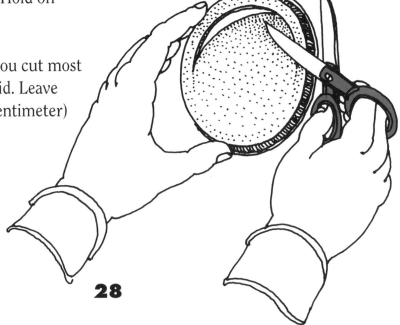

Pilots often use a wind sock to show them exactly which way the wind is blowing. It helps them decide how to take off and land their planes.

You can make a wind-finder that works just like a wind sock. Hold on to your hat and try it.

1. Ask a grown-up to help you cut most of the center out of the lid. Leave about a 1/4-inch (.625-centimeter) rim.

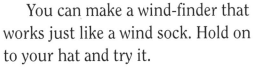

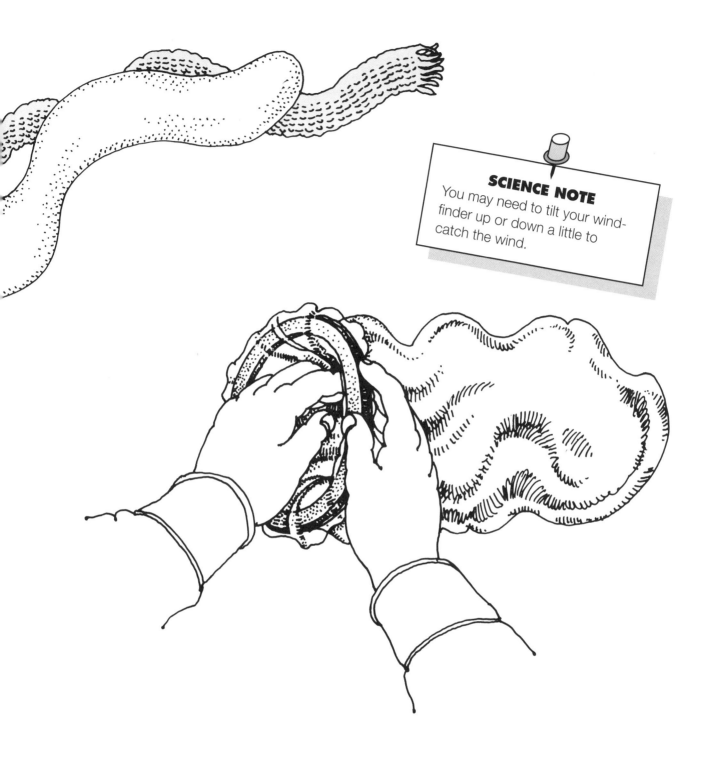

SCIENCE NOTE
You may need to tilt your wind-finder up or down a little to catch the wind.

2. Pull the open end of the bag through the lid and turn it back over the rim. Tape the edges to the sides of the bag.

3. Cut a hole about the size of a quarter in the bottom of the bag.

4. Take your wind-finder outside when the wind is blowing. Hold it over your head by the lid's rim, with the large opening at the front.

5. Turn around slowly. Watch what happens when your wind-finder faces exactly into the wind.

Take a Spin

YOU NEED:

★ Modeling clay
★ An unsharpened pencil
★ A flashlight
★ A dark room

Did you ever think you could spin around and around without getting dizzy? Well, that's what happens to you every day and every night. You take a big spin—as big as the planet Earth itself. You see daytime and nighttime because Earth is turning, and you go along for the ride!

Find out for yourself how Earth spins. Then try to imagine what it would be like if the planet stopped spinning.

1. Roll a piece of modeling clay into a ball.

2. Carefully push the pencil through the ball of clay. You may have to squeeze the clay around the ball to hold it in place.

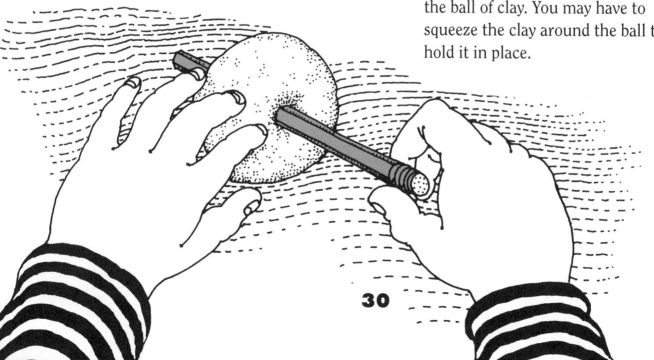

3. Pretend the ball is Earth. Use a pencil or pen to make a small *x* in the ball. This shows the place where you live.

4. Have a friend or a grown-up help you. Take the ball and the flashlight into a dark room.

5. Pretend the flashlight is the sun. Have your helper turn it on and shine it on "Earth." What part of Earth is light? What part is dark?

6. Turn "Earth" slowly and watch what happens where you live. When is it daytime? When is it night? How does it get to be day again?

SCIENCE NOTE
Earth rotates—it spins like a top. It makes one complete rotation every day.

What if Earth didn't spin and it had one "day side" and one "night side"? Which side would you rather live on? Tell a story or draw pictures to show how your life would be if you lived where it was always day or always night.